Zenith in Quasar

Fatima Amin

ISBN 978-93-5458-545-6

Published in India 2021 by Pencil

A brand of
One Point Six Technologies Pvt. Ltd.
123, Building J2, Shram Seva Premises,
Wadala Truck Terminal, Wadala (E)
Mumbai 400037, Maharashtra, INDIA
E connect@thepencilapp.com
W www.thepencilapp.com

Author biography

Grinding Word's author, Fatima Amin writes sweet, fun, and soothing poetries. Her tales are motivating and fearless, but in real life, Fatima is afraid of basements, fake friends, and going up stairs when it is dark.

Fatima is best known for her recent book, Unheard Musings. She has been a part and a junior writer at The Literary. Society of India and is designated as The Literary Lieutenant at StoryMirror. Her other talents counts photography, tattoo designing and urdu poetries.

CONTENTS

Epigraph

To love and to be loved.

Foreword

In her recently book Unheard Musings, author Fatima wrote a deeply insightful foreword that shares her feelings about the book, its inspiration, and its goals. Here is an excerpt:

A poet is the only one who truly knows it. They sew exquisite poems with tiny words with a pinch of realism and imagination. Not everyone can be a writer, but if you're trying to be the one then write your thoughts, time to act, pen it fast, write it down before it fades. Write the words before the time's up.

Preface

Most of the beautiful poetries in this book really occurred, almost each are experience of my own.
This book is designed to sink a shaft to a lost souls.

Acknowledgements

For this book, I wanna thank the love of my life for always motivating me enough to fight obstacles, for making me who I am and for believing in me.

Introduction

A poetry collection consist of love and commitments within two souls. It's hard to forget the first love , but more harder to love again and when you fall there's no going backs.

The person

I am not the person I used to be
I am a graveyard of all the emotions
I once used to feel.

Peace

As an autistic woman,away from the world as a woman buried among feelings I am learning and understanding.

Understanding

I can hear you I can understand you
without words without sounds.

Darling

And darling,you were my first love before being the last.

Craving

I'm craving for his lovelike a word block to a poet inking a beautiful poem.

Being hollowed

Regret sometimes hollows a person from inside

why we should do such a thing which we have to repent after doing.

Love

With eyes eager to search,
thumping and calming
gleaming and smiling
hoping and seeking

as I see the twilight.

Hope

You cast a spell on me with your hand
that feeds a little bird,

You made me write again with your smile
that brought me hope.

His hands

We are correct to place our faith in his hands.

He cups it,
as if it were a bird bound for freedom.

And nurtures it,

till it's old enough to move mountains.

The moon's art

Her lunar rays makes your eyes pop,
like a celestial eyeliner.
While it brings a serene blush upon your cheeks.
You become her art,
as she blesses you with her makeup.

Fix me

Fix me not because I'm broken

fix me because you love me for who I am.

Saranghae

He is my every sip of coffee,
he makes me feel so high and energetic.
Where he makes me addictive towards him.

Even as a kid

From childhood to days unknown

we'll cherish always the joy you've shown.

Never before

Of all the sweetest little things
you'll never know what joy you bring.

A thousand thoughts, a million more
we've never known such joy before.

Dusk and dawn

Let my love snuggle him
as he naps each night.
Let his worries fly away,
as he wakes each day.

Devil within him

The devil with a friendly face
makes my heart race.
I live life in fear like I scream everywhere
but no one wants to hear.

Paint me, my love

Like how you artistically
spill some coffee in your sleeve.

Paint me, my love,

with your yellow aura in a blue sunday

with your warm smiles in a cold day.
Paint me, my love,

with your crystal tears in the darkest days
with your sparkling smile in hardest days.

Your love

And i'll treasure these colors,
engraved in my skin

as if they are my precious stones.

Excerpt

You painted daisies on my skin
when I swear it felt like spring,

but autumn was just around the corner
and everything was perfectly placed.

Hugsy

I still wish to cuddle.
To your body instead of the lifeless Teddy Bear
That has been lying next to me in the bed,

after you left.

The night

Lately you're all I think,
our disaster comes to mind.

Your face pops up when I blink,
so beautiful like no kind.

Is this love or is this hollow?
Will we ever know?
I don't care, I'll just follow
Let's just take it slow.

This came out of nothing,
without anybody knowing
it turned into loving,
without a certain going.

She and He

Whatever she thought,
I thought about it next.
She said I might be able to read her mind.
She could throw anything into this universe,
and I will catch them all pretty much instantly.

Dreams

If I get lost in between the
cobwebs and forgotten dreams
please, come for me.

Heavens cooperated

Oh! how I have dreamed,
of days like this
full of laughter, fun nights intertwined.

Oh! how I have dreamed!
of nights like this,
having fun in our merry ways.

I wish

I wish you and I walk on a bridge
entwined hands,
winds steal our hearts.

Moonlight fill our empty minds
silence relax our dwindled skin.

Embedded wishes in the sky
melt on our lips,
earth's revolution exclude all turmoils.

We float with cold breeze of nights;
and unread poetries.

Pain

Once you endure pain till last.
The next you won't feel it,

rest you will enjoy.

Give up

As long as you don't give up

you can still be saved.

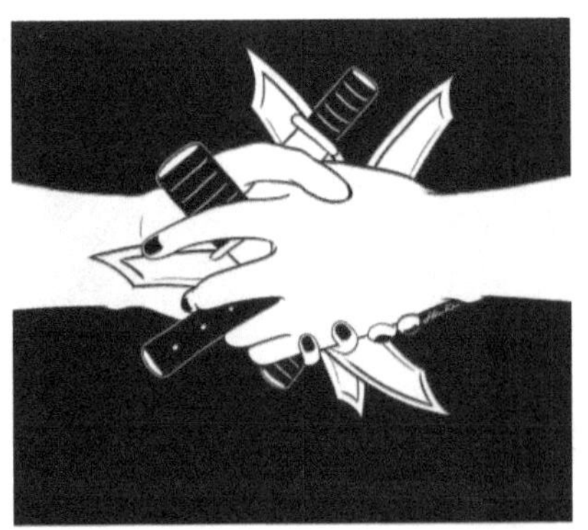

Feel

I shut down my eyes

I can feel his hand in mine
arms muffled around me.
Hands gently touching against mine

head composed with his thoughts.

Sinner

Tragedies of a beguiled beauty

trapped in lustrous temptation.

Her lure is so deadly that even
the devil carries vary reservations.

Our talks

We will touch our breaths
frozen in mid-air with silent fingertips.
And watch them disintegrate
into the pauses of our conversations.

Thee and me

If there is even a semblance of thee and me
I'll fold this possibility inside layers of sapphire satin,
and hide us within the deepest recess of me.

Enigma

YOU'RE AN ENIGMA;
YOU BREAK MY HEART IN TWO
THEN PIECE IT TOGETHER
WITH YOUR WICKED TONGUE.

Forever

You are that story I wanna complete
with favourable ending.

Eternity

From now until the end of time
we'll hold onto your joy sublime.

Write

Some men write like their hands is on fire
some men write down the whispers of their demons, some
men write for the woman they kiss

some men write to give hope for the next generation.

Look into my eyes

WHEN I LOOK INTO YOUR EYES
I SEE YOUR SOUL, PARADISE, AN ANGEL SYMPHONY. LOOK INTO MY EYES, I FORESEE YOU WILL FIND YOUR UNIVERSE WITHIN ME.

Redolent

You remind me of a restful summer's eve

after a hot and humid summer day,
of a cool breeze that blows carefree

with it taking all of life's troubles away.

Reminder

You remind of the ocean vast

near a sandy, pebbled beach,

A colourful kite traversing the skies

within yet out of reach.

Moonlit sky

You make me remember the moon
sIlent, serene yet ablaze,
with rays of white lights

leaving me forever amazed.

Language bino

It is a broken language.
A sought after appeal
a cry for justice in twisted tongue.

A beam of hope
when its source was common indignation
and a character of purity,
only tarnished by an upset mindset.

Extinguish

So here we are once more
stirring a pit with no content.
Mala fide, not knowing where to hide our faith,

except in bubbles of thoughts
we heavily wish to extinguish.

Attention

When he came near to me
I felt like I was slapped
with a bunch of lavender.

where I am his gardener,
harvesting his attention.

Leave

I never asked you to stay,
because I never thought you would leave.

Ebony

Decked in shades of ebony I live

enveloped in the darkness of the night,
yet my lucid dreams are filled with

festering images in pristine white.

World's eye

There's a graveyard in my heart,
with bodies lying deep inside.
They are of no one else but me
buried deep down away from world's eyes.

Offer

I offered him a shoulder to lean onthough I know he will fight alone.I offered him my heart to stay inthough I know he will stay elsewhere.

www.ingramcontent.com/pod-product-compliance
Lightning Source LLC
LaVergne TN
LVHW050423160726
843469LV00041B/1214

9789354585456